WALKING ON THE BLADE

poems

Maria Mimi Molori

mimipublishing

Mimi Publishing
Stonington CT 06378

Published 2009
Published in the United States of America

Illustrations, from istock.com, are used by permission.
Book design by Marie A Carija

ISBN 978-0-578-03015-9

To the two best things in my life...my Larry and my K

SPECIAL ACKNOWLEDGEMENTS

To my 7th grade teacher, Ms. Mary Margaret Quinn. When I went back to visit her in my freshman year of high school to read her some of my poems, she said, "you have a gift here, young lady."

To Porf. The realities of youth, SMH and beyond, belong only to us....

The BIGGEST thank you is to Robin, my soul-mate, my friend, my sister, who has supported me 100% plus in any venture I have pursued.

To Marie, who when I went to her office with my ideas for this book, responded to me and my poems with such positive feedback. She had some fabulous ideas—giving me added confidence and the push to "keep on trucking." I will be forever grateful, thank you.

And there are also those who never had faith in me or my voice. This short but unique statement from my friend David is for them: "Mimi, you are an enigma…wrapped up in a mystery."

INTRODUCTION

Walking on the Blade consists of poems I started writing at the age of fourteen on the beautiful shoreline of Salisbury Beach in Massachusetts where I spent every summer at my grandparents' cottage until the age of twenty-five.

I would be walking along the ocean and get into a deep-thought type of mood. Being so young, I didn't realize my thoughts were coming together to write a poem.... So one day—I had some paper and a pen in my beach bag—I sat on the sand and I wrote my first poem, "Sadness." As time went on I totally understood that unique feeling and what it meant. It became my own special time. No one ever knew about it. I figured that no one would even begin to understand it, so why even try?

When I recently told my dear friend Joyce, whom I have known my entire life, that I was going to publish my poems, she said, "I didn't even know you wrote poems." My cousin Jamie—as kids we were partners in crime—recently read a few of my poems and started to cry, hugged me and said, "they say so much about you."

Mimi Molori
Stonington, CT
June, 2009

Walking on the Blade

Radiant

The relief of tension
and emotion,
makes a new person.
A burst of light,
a feeling of peace.
I am now experiencing
total optimism.
I had to believe I could
become stronger.
I needed all these traits
to make my life
a glowing reality.

Her Unfinished Life

Her friends find her spunky
But she finds herself rather dull.
She doesn't know why that is so.
She wasn't happy with what she had.
She puts on a front, a smile with her friends.
That is why they thought she had a complete life.
She must learn, if you push, strive
and achieve what you want,
then your life won't ever be unfinished.

Dreams

Dreams make up most of me,
they make me try to achieve
my goals in life.
I often dream of the future.
What will I be?
What will I have become?
But most of all, will I be alive
to keep trying?
This is what I often dream of,
will I succeed?
Will I reach the top of my mountain
of dreams???

Forgetting How To Write

Forgetting how to write worries me.
It worries me to think I've lost
something I once treasured.
It makes me wonder what writing
is all about.
To have the ability to express your
feelings and emotions on a
piece of paper.
Writing makes you realize the true
meaning of all your thoughts.
Writing is thinking on paper.
So maybe I haven't really forgotten
how to write, maybe it's only
another special thought…

The Flow

The flow of words with quality and a similar
connection comes very quickly to me. I must
get to them fast, or they disappear.
I grab a pen, paper, and a poem begins, so
cool and calmly, from my brain, through my
heart, thru my pen, onto a piece of paper.
How a small, simple "flow" ends with such a
HUGE smile on my face, can't ever be told.

The Block

Writer's block sucks...
If the mood isn't there, the poem isn't there.
It is due to the frustrations, rushing and worrying
of life and love. Writing scopes out your precious
thoughts and shuts out the rest of the world,
The moment is only yours.
When the block is there, a crowded, humid swelling
engulfs you; You cannot be seen or heard. Pens and
paper are demons to you. Walk away and have
them come to you, at that cherished time.

Time

I haven't had time to write,
or should I say, I haven't
wanted to find the time.
I'm scared, scared of the
feelings I may express
through writing.
By avoiding certain issues,
life can be strange and confusing.
I should stop being senseless
and face it.
Now is my time to write
and express all those complex
feelings inside of me...

What's Wrong With Me?

Am I just tired or just giving up?
Do I know what's right or wrong?
Am I still confident enough to be the "real" me?
Do I exaggerate or underestimate?
Am I great in my own eyes or am I ugly?
Will I make it, make it through
this period of "inner war" or
will I burst within the little peace I have???

The Gift of Hope

Hopes comes in short baby steps, 10 forward then 6 back.
It never last too long, snatch it up and run quickly with it.
The marathon of hope begins. You don't need to win the race,
Just cross the finish line, so your "hope" becomes the rare gift
of a dream come true.

Two Dark, Frightening Storms

Looking out my bedroom window, I see frightened,
tiny raindrops clinging to each other for protection.
One of their worst enemies is the howling wind,
pushing and pulling these tiny raindrops apart.
Then looking high into the sky, they see tiny white clouds
running as fast as they can from the "big, mean, black cloud"
chasing them farther and farther apart.
I am like the raindrops, trying to be strong, in my own little
way. I am running from something big and dark.
Something that said it would "chase me forever"…
It is pulling and pushing me apart from the two most
important things in my life.
One very different thing from the clouds, raindrops and
wind, they know what they're doing and they know where
to run and hide.
I do not know where to run and hide or how he is going
to "wrongly strike again."
I do not know how to get my two treasures back, from one
"VERY DARK, FRIGHTENING STORM"…

To My Dear Bitch Of An Algebra Teacher

I despise you, that's if you don't
already know.
You conduct a zoo, not a class.
You are the zookeeper and we
your students are monkeys.
You make the average student feel like an imbecile
You make the bright student feel like a god.
In your class I feel like a piece of cheese
ready to be consumed by a pack of mice.
I am lost...
I don't appreciate your method of teaching.
So speaking for the entire class,
Dear Bitch of an Algebra Teacher,
Please Drop Dead...

Poor Michael (In memory of Diane)

Poor Michael, confused, lonely and tired.
What happens when total depression
hovers over your entire being???
He wants to live, he wants to die,
poor Michael.
He doesn't know which way to turn,
all he goes through is suffering.
What Michael can't realize is life has
ups and downs.
If Michael could realize this,
then none of us would have to say,
poor, poor Michael...

What Do You Do?

When you don't know where you are
and you don't know what you're doing?
When you reach out to love
and no one is there?
When you call and no one answers?
When silence hovers over all?
When society booms and you fail?
When you walk on an endless road
and you fall one million times?
What do you do?
Do you still keep trying or give up,
give up the life you once loved?
N-E-V-E-R ! ! !

Sadness

Sadness is a time of a person's life,
when he is totally alone, totally helpless.
His heart is broken and only
a friend can mend it.
He feels extinct, his life is a timeless
place of mourn.
His life is barren, cold and lonely,
if he only had a friend.
Sadness causes depression, a lack of
living, a lack of life.
Sadness to me can not be controlled, it
can only be conquered.
Happiness is great but when you don't
have that you're in limbo.
If only a friend notices his sadness and
tries to encourage
a person sure of himself and sure of the
outside world.
Someone please help him, help him
become alive, help him become a unit
within himself.
To believe he is truly beautiful and unique.
Because all of us are truly beautiful and unique.

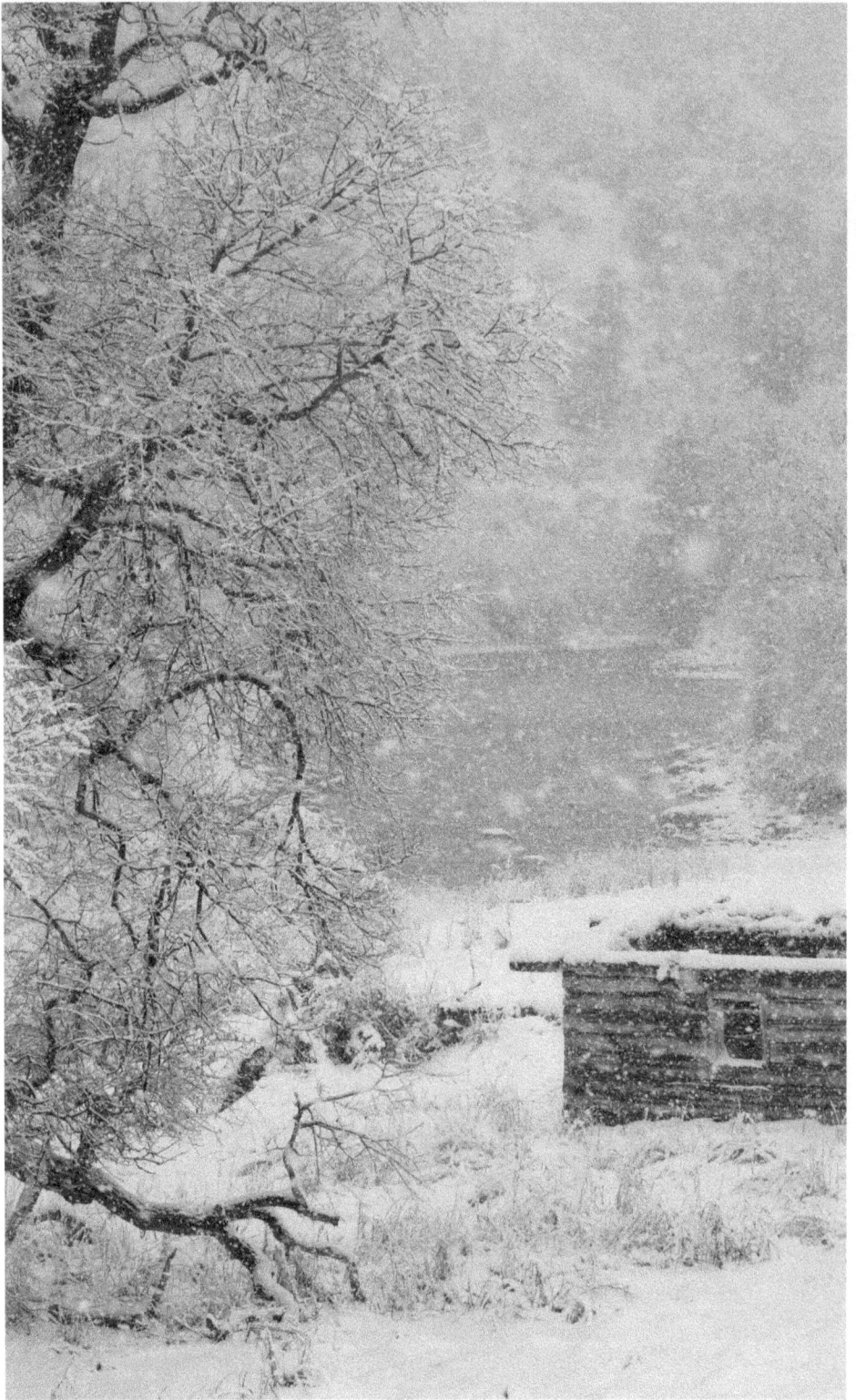

It's Here Again

That rotten, unpredictable, confused feeling.
It has all different names, call it what you want.
But I don't like it, I'm scared, it frightens me.
Now that this time is here, I say and do all the
wrong things and I feel all the wrong ways.
Hoping these feelings leave soon,
I often think of the other world,
and if it really is a paradise…
But I'll be there forever, never to return to
this rotten, unpredictable, confused feeling.
It's here again...............

If I Were Dead

If I were dead, I wouldn't have to live in a
world full of hate and sneaks.
What a world, what a time of life,
everything turns out wrong.
If I were dead, I wouldn't have to be
in this state, this state of depression.
Oh someone please help, I don't know what's
wrong but something is wrong.
Help Me Before I Am Dead...

No Reason To Live

If I knew someone needed me, or wanted me,
then maybe I would have a reason to live.
I know no one wants me and I know no one needs me.
I have no purpose in life,
so it is time I leave this life...

The World Today

Where are you?
If you can find yourself in it,
then maybe, just maybe,
you were really sent by God.

Stillness

Silence is what it's all about,
It has no meaning or no real purpose.
"I have no real purpose,"
I'm just here and there.
People can also just exist,
by the loss of words.
Let me think and try to recall
what I am all about…???
Let all people recapture their lives
and help bring back a "whole populace"
of determined strivers for a better life…

No One

No one to smile or laugh with.
No one to love or care for.
No one to warm or hug you.
No one to cherish or depend on.
No one, no one at all,
not even someone to cry to...

I'm Back, Brother

Brother I had an awful time.
But now I'm back.
Back where I belong.
I bet you thought,
I deserted you.
It was really tough,
all those different people,
ideas, concepts, and ways.
I didn't know where to go.
I didn't know who to talk to.
I should have come to you.
I took the wrong road, but
that doesn't count anymore.
I found that right road, Jesus
and that right road is you...

Calvary

To set a goal and watch it splash.
To dream and have it crash.
To build a wall and watch it collapse.
To wake up in the morning with a smile
and go to bed at night with the taste of bile.
Remembering Christ was nailed to the
cross will make my splash, crash,
collapse and bile experiences to become
stronger and bring me closer to God.

Loveless

The willingness to love
is an intolerable situation.
Just hoping to be wanted
and accepted for what you
are can be an impossibility.
Give up on love or it will
fall down on you.

People

Questioning, anxious to grow, thrilling,
willing to stand together, willing to stand alone.
Ready for anything, acceptance is widely thrown.
You have a friend if you only call.
Suspense withdraws from all.
In the last analysis, all a person needs
for survival are people...

Are There Any Friends?

Today I realized I have no friends at all.
I am alone, I have been abandoned by
the people I thought were friends.
I am left alone this entire weekend.
There isn't anyone to call or talk to.
I have been rejected like a disease.
No one will associate with me.
Is there such a thing as a friend?
It is a world of jealous sneaks and bitches.
All my so called "friends" would be
delighted to know I was alone.
I can make it alone, I will survive.
I will keep on dreaming until I find
just one true friend to enjoy "a reality" with...

Friends

I thought I had friends, I guess I don't.
The only friend I have is the radio.
I don't like this lonely feeling, I am afraid of it.
It haunts me, it scares me and it just
might be the end of me.

Use Me

You use me for a walk, for a smile.
You use me for all you can.
You act as if we are one and I am your world.
The comical thing about all this is, I use you,
as you use me....

We Are Over

We have ended.
What a time.
It's all so very strange.
Just as a rainbow appears
with power to make you quiver,
it will disappear right in front
of your eyes leaving your heart,
your soul and mind,
so very, very barren…

Being The Fool

Everybody is a fool once in a lifetime.
I guess my role of the fool is being acted now.
I am a fool and completely exhausted.
My mind is totally worn out from thinking of him.
I cannot believe we are really over
and I am really the fool.
I should have known it was coming,
but Love is blind and I couldn't see.
Everybody plays a fool and I am now on stage
as the FOOL...

Saying Nothing

Saying nothing is what it was all about...
he wanted that.
Writing on lines, words that left no meaning or no real purpose...
he wanted that.
I had no "real purpose," I was just here and there...
he wanted that.
My words were just space eaters and space savers, words that
could ramble on and on forever and ever...
he wanted that.
People can also ramble on forever, not by words, but by the
loss of words, rambling in turmoil.
Let us think and recall to mind what are we three all about???
Let us recapture our lives and bring back a "whole unity"
of three determined strivers for a better life.
...HE DOES NOT WANT THAT...

The Feeling Of Love

Love is an emotion, a feeling when
you don't know what is happening
to your whole being.
Your mind and body are transformed
into clouds of joy.
You don't realize it is love,
because there are times love cannot
be defined.
You just know it is the greatest
feeling in the world.
When you have this feeling, try to
hold onto it as tightly as you can,
because you will be able to define love
when you no longer have it...

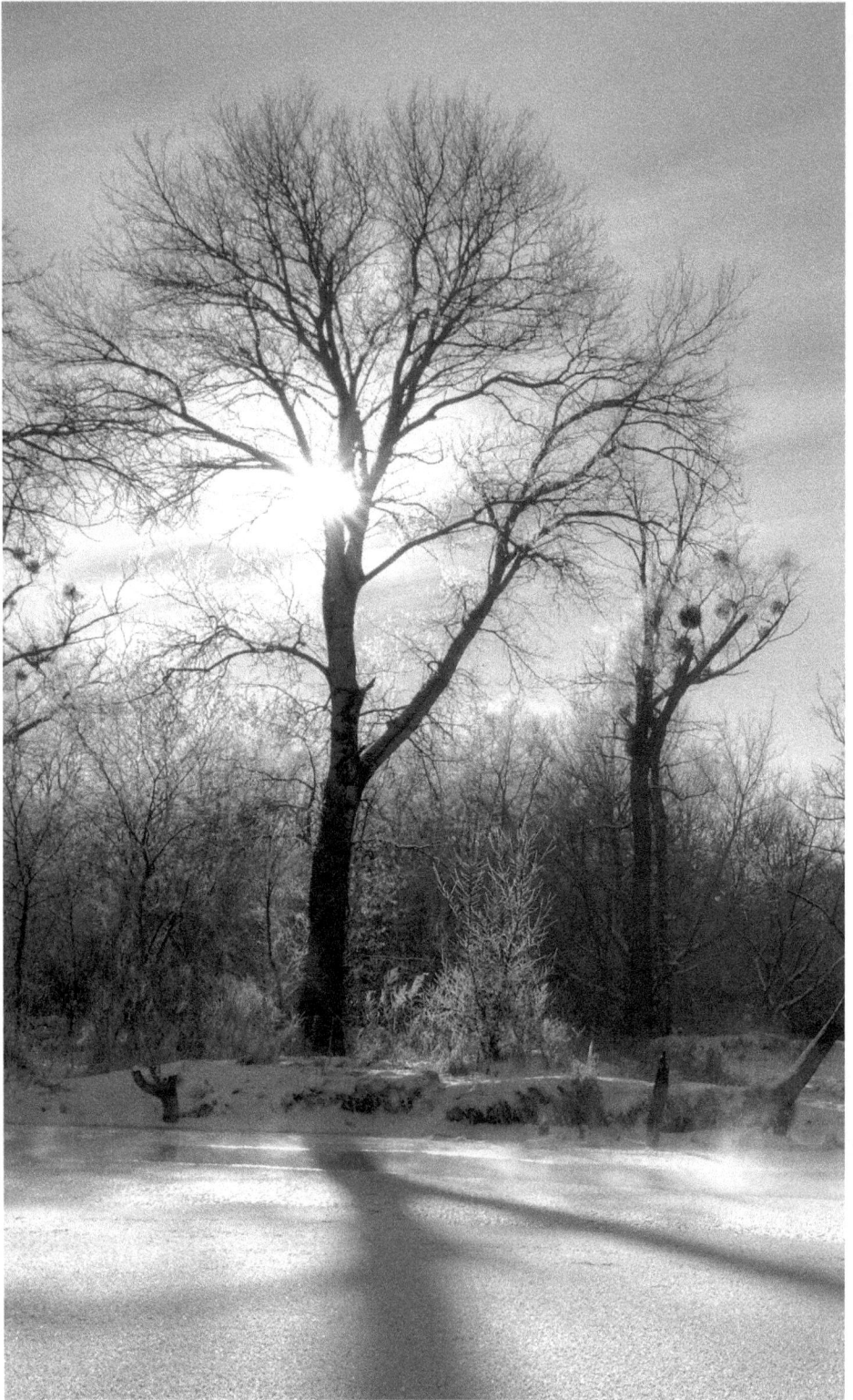

The Gift Of Love

When you receive the gift of love it is
a holiday to celebrate for as long as you have it.
You want to keep it and treasure it forever.
The feeling you get is one of security and warmth.
It's only when you don't have the gift of love
that there is no holiday to celebrate.

That Special Boy Up The Street

That special boy made me feel special.
He made me feel like a real woman.
My heart jumped a beat when he spoke to me.
I don't know his name, I only know
he lives up the street.
I walked to the park with him, we talked
in a very special way.
Oh, that special boy up the street
is very special to me.

Our Thrill

We were happy together, we smiled, we loved.
We could walk and not speak, our hands together spoke for us.
Now, NO smiles, NO love. When we walk we are terrified of the
silence, because our hands NO longer speak.
WHAT THRILL?????

Have We Made It?

Have we made it, through the dark age?
The dark age of finding out?
Have we realized our true feelings
for one another?
Have we adapted ourselves to each other's good
and bad habits?
Have we accepted each other for what
we really are?
Or are we strangers just pretending
to love?
Or are we dreaming all is just fine?
Let's continue trying until we
believe we have made it...

Ask Me If I Need You

If I could give you all your dreams and wishes, I would.
If I could let you be happy and successful, I would.
If I could make every day the sunniest day, I would.
If I could make the stars dance for you, I would.
If I could do all these things for you, just to
let you need me as I need you, I would.
If I could possibly do all this for you in one tiny lifespan,
I would…

Inspiration

An inspiration of love inspires all
you come in contact with.
Glowing vibrations flow from within,
to touch the hearts of all.
Those whose hearts you do not touch
are afraid to love.
Their inspiration is frustration...

KING HEROIN

King Heroin is the mightiest ruler of all.
He conquers your mind, body, and soul.
He is very thorough when it comes to you...
You never know just when he will strike,
you only know he's there.
He is always VICTORIOUS.
He is absolute ruler of YOU...
King Heroin is a bizarre and creepy "THING."
Different, huh???
King Heroin, even though you behave as a cruel,
ruthless and brutal king,
I will never be a property of your domain...

Turning Point

What a fuckin time, it's really
the turning point.
Everything and everyone is so screwed up.
Everyone is constantly stoned,
what's going to happen?
God help them all to straighten out,
before there will be no way to
straighten me out...

Love

Love is intricate.
Love is sorrowful.
Love is life.
Life is full of love.
Love is people.
People are love.
Love is you, and
you are my love…

Rain

Rain gets me in a thinking mood.
Rain makes me think of you.
You make me think of love and of life.
Rain is a time I treasure very much.

Peace, What Is It?

Peace, a beautiful thing.
I often think of true peace.
Peace is something none
of us knows of.
Peace, a beautiful thing.
A thing of life.
A thing of people.
We must obtain peace.
All we see now is depression,
poverty, starving people and
dying soldiers.
Peace must come, it has to come
If peace doesn't come, we'll have
to go to peace.
Peace, a beautiful thing…

ABOUT THE AUTHOR

Maria Molori, known to most of her friends as "Mimi," is a member of the American Poets Society and is anticipating an invitation to read at the lovely Hill-Stead Museum Sunken Garden Poetry Festival in Farmington, Connecticut.

Mimi is an avid ocean-lover. Her close friends say she is part mermaid. She has her boater's license and buzzes around the water and coves of her beautiful Stonington Borough neighborhood in Connecticut. She enjoys lobster so much that in 2005 she got her lobster license. She puts her lobster traps out in May by the rocks in a cove that is her front yard, and they stay there until October.... Mimi does need help pulling up the traps to collect the lobsters a couple of times a week. Her joke is, it's so she won't break her lovely finger nails, but the truth is, they are too heavy for her to lift alone....

She rescues all her dogs. Her newest darling is a Westie named Thistle. A women's advocate, she works with battered women and inner city teens.

The most wonderful miracles and the greatest joys in her life are her two daughters, Laura and Kristen. Mimi says the two days they were born were both days of marvelous amazement—no other days in her life can compare.... They are grown young women today, and she is honored to be their mom.

Journal

*Use the following pages to make notes
for your own journey
of self-discovery.*

Journal

Journal

Journal

Journal

Journal

Journal